CH00405736

DASTRAM / DELIRIU

Alasdair Mac Mhaighstir Alasdair (c.1698-c.1770) was a Scottish Gaelic poet, lexicographer, military officer, and Gaelic language tutor to Charles Edward Stuart, popularly known as Bonnie Prince Charlie. Little of his life can be confirmed aside from his role as a teacher in Scotland's Ardnamurchan peninsula, and as a captain in the Clanranald regiment of the 1745 rebellion. His only volume of poetry, the self-published *Aiseirigh na Seann Chànain Albannaich* (1751), was the first secular work to be published in any of the Celtic languages. As a teacher, he compiled and published the first Gaelic-English dictionary. Alasdair's reputation has stirred controversy, his book reputedly having been burnt in Edinburgh after its publication.

Taylor Strickland is a poet and translator from the US. He is the author of *Commonplace Book* and *Dastram/Delirium*. His poem 'The Low Road' was adapted by American composer, Andrew Kohn, and performed in Orkney. His poem 'Nine Whales, Tiree' is in the process of being adapted to film with filmmaker Olivia Booker and composer Fee Blumenthaler. He is currently a doctoral candidate in literary translation at the University of Glasgow, and he lives in Glasgow, with his wife, Lauren.

Also by Taylor Strickland

Commonplace Book (Broken Sleep Books, 2022)

Dastram / Delirium

Alasdair Mac Mhaighstir Alasdair **/** Taylor Strickland

ISBN: 978-1-915760-11-1

The author has asserted their right to be identified as the author of this Work in accordance with the Copyright, Designs and Patents Act 1988

Cover designed by Aaron Kent

Edited & Typeset by Aaron Kent

Broken Sleep Books Ltd
Rhydwen
Talgarreg
Ceredigion
SA44 4HB

Broken Sleep Books Ltd
Fair View
St Georges Road
Cornwall
PL26 7YH

Contents

What follows is a subversive translation of poetry by the 18th-century Scottish Gaelic poet, Alasdair Mac Mhaighstir Alasdair. What is 'subversive translation'? Originally a term used by Rody Gorman when making his own translations of Mac Mhaighstir Alasdair, subversion is less a technical methodology and more an accountability act that represents a text through translation, but which accepts the failure in worthwhile translation as sufficient in its own right. 'Worthwhile translation' is what is being subverted. Gorman claims Alasdair's sonic system is 'impossible... to replicate in another language'.[1] If true, worthwhile translation is a pretense that glosses over complexity:

> 'S thadhlamaid san fhrìth,
> 'S chailleamaid sinn fhìn
> Feadh na' srònagan

These three lines alone from the first stanza of the poem 'Moladh Mòraig' demonstrate intricately knitted internal rhyme, conditional forms, emphatic forms, and a word 'frìth' whose meaning is untranslatable in English, and which, in this case, carries a pun that is also untranslatable. 'Frìth' is often rendered 'deer forest' but said forest is, in the Highland Scottish setting, where this poem takes place, better described as a moorland, one set aside for hunting deer. In medieval England there were 'deer parks', or nowadays 'game reserves', but neither of those capture the right ecological connotation. Then there is the pun. Pronounced a bit like the English word 'free', the 'frìth' was on the outer edges of civil society, and Mac Mhaighstir Alasdair being a fluent English-speaker likely meant this to be a double entendre. The frìth was the one place to which he and his lover could abscond and be free of the eyes of

1   Gorman, Rody. *Alasdair MacDonald's Relocation from Eigneig to Inverie: A Contemporary Poet's Attempt at Subversive translation.* ed. Camille Dressler and D.W. Stiubhart. 'Alexander MacDonald: Bard of the Gaelic Enlightenment.' The Islands Book Trust, 2012, South Lochs, Isle of Lewis. p. 70

societal judgement. Alasdair's poetry, according to Gorman, then, resists worthwhile translation because it is 'so language-specific'.[2] Gaelic has an extreme concreteness and its emphatic forms are inimitable in English writing; if translation is limited in ability, perhaps counterintuitively subversive translation does wrong in order to do right:

> We took off
> like deer over the deer-moor,
> deep into headlands.
> We got lost. We got so lost.

Liberties have been taken, of course, but Mac Mhaighstir Alasdair's voice and the core of his poetics have been preserved. To what end? How does this differ from Lowell's imitations or Dryden's paraphrase? A strong ethics emerges here. Susan Sontag thought of literary translation as an '[extension of] our sympathies... to secure and deepen the awareness (with all its consequences) that other people... really do exist.'[3] Mac Mhaighstir Alasdair and the Gaelic for which he so determinedly laboured have too often been marginalized, or at best anthologized, in English. Even his name is better known in translation as 'Alexander MacDonald'. Even that name is hardly known. This book, with all its consequences, aims to deepen our awareness in English of Alasdair Mac Mhaighstir Alasdair.

Chan eil ach beagan Gàidhlig agam... (I do not have but a little Gaelic...) I am therefore indebted to the help of Gillebrìde MacMillan, and I have often resorted to previous translations by Pàdraig MacAoidh and Iain S MacPherson, Ronald Black, Michael Newton, John Lorne Campbell and Gordon Barr. All mistakes are my own.

---

2   Ibid.
3   Sontag, Susan. *The World as India*. susansontag.com/prize/on-Translation.shtml

Foreword

Alasdair Mac Mhaighstir Alasdair, or at any rate Alexander MacDonald, should be a household name like Robert Burns in Scotland but far from it. An eighteenth-century poet, born in Moidart, his poetry was passionate, innovative, inventive, transgressive, equalled for its power only by the poetry of Sorley MacLean in the 20th century. Of course, the circulation of MacDonald's poetry furth of the Highlands was limited by its minority-language status but neither was it served well by its early translators who expurgated and prettified it.

MacDonald's life is often presented as one of contradictions, but poetry thrives on paradox. He started life as an Episcopalian, became a Presbyterian in the pay of an organisation whose express purpose had been to stamp out Gaelic, and later a Catholic and a captain in Bonnie Prince Charlie's army. He was the author of the first two secular books published in Gaelic and introduced new themes from English and the Classics while incorporating anachronisms and teaching himself insular miniscule in order to read medieval Gaelic texts. He attended Glasgow University and was open to the science of the Enlightenment while being willing to die for a dynasty that went back to Clann Mhíl and Scota, Pharaoh's daughter.

Although a modern edition and translation of his complete works is still to be published, sections of his work have appeared in recent years with various approaches to translation ranging from scanning cribs to spirited reimaginings. Strickland's versions belong to the latter type. They constitute a long selection from the poem 'Moladh Mòraig', which describes fornication *al fresco*, and shorter selections from three other poems or songs, one Jacobite, one in praise of Sugar Brook and its environs, and the third, a piece of bawdry. Knowing the poems in Gaelic, I inevitably miss certain aspects of the originals. I miss the sea dyed the colour of oranges and Lili who would be perfect but for her white eyelashes; I miss the delicious naturalness of his love-making, the tripping rhythms of trisyllables and his self-parodying strings of alliterating, new-coined adjectives.

But Strickland's versions do not set out to be line-by-line translations; rather, their authority lies in their intensity of response. He often repurposes or alters the images of the originals in slightly different contexts to recapture and condense MacDonald's mercurial thought, outrageousness and irony, his word-play and mix of register. The whole point is that Strickland's versions are contemporary American poetry, his inter-sexual tilting less earthy and more edgy than MacDonald's. And isn't that what a version should be – an off-spring, born live and free and crying out with poetic conviction?

— *Meg Bateman, Sabhal Mòr Ostaig, 2023*

Praised Be Morag

—

bho Moladh Mòraig

Ùrlar

Pity not being in the wood.
When Morag was there
we joined those sunny bonny
brown-haired girls
for a laugh, guessing the cutest of us,
a coin toss to know.
Yet we outshined them all,
immortalized among wild rose—
on our stomachs, lying to each other,
lying to ourselves.
Our playfight became our foreplay.
Our sun cups delicately
picked from split rock. We took off
like deer over the deer-moor,
deep into headlands.
We got lost. We got so lost.

Ùrlar

'S truagh gun mi sa choill'
Nuair bha Mòrag ann,
Thilgeamaid na cruinn
Cò bu bhòidhch' againn;
Inghean a' chùil dhuinn
Air a bheil a loinn,
Bhiomaid air ar broinn
Feadh na' ròsanan;
Bhreugamaid sinn fhìn,
Mireag air ar blìon,
A' buain shòbhrach mìn-bhuidh'
Na' còsagan;
Theannamaid ri strì
'S thadhlamaid san fhrìth,
'S chailleamaid sinn fhìn
Feadh na' srònagan

Ùrlar

Eyes like blue dewberry
in a film of dawn,
her facial blush lovely
as flowering citrus;
as flour stoneground
her powdery top, and under—
her soft pubic song.
She is sun and center
to our planetary orbit.
Star untarnished,
Vesta among virgins.
Despite all other leading lights,
only in her, a mirror,
can beauty self-identify.
Flower that stirs,
jewel that blazes sight.
Morag is human clay?
I cannot believe my eyes.

Ùrlar

Sùil mar ghorm-dhearc driùchd
Ann an ceò-mhadainn,
Deirg' is gil' nad ghnùis
Mar bhlàth òirseidean;
Shuas cho mìn ri plùr,
Shìos garbh mo chulaidh-chiùil,
Grian na planaid-cùrs'
Am measg òigheannan;
Reula glan gun smùr
Measg na' rionnag-iùil,
Sgàthan-mais' air flùr
Na bòidhchid thu;
Àilleagan glan ùr
A dhallas ruisg gu 'n cùl;
Mas ann do chrèadhaich thù
'S adhbhar mòr-iongnaidh.

Ùrlar

Not since I first rooked
into manhood, coming-of-age,
have I laid eyes on so fine a thing.
There were others, of course,
like gentle Maili
whose smile filled with rowanberry.
But she only sang
capricious airs. Peigi was too late
in years, otherwise
she would have had my heart.
Marsaili, however… not quite there,
yet always there. A nutter.
Lili's eyelids glowed
but she, nor any other, has the deeper
stare that Morag has—a stare
warm enough to bathe in.

Ùrlar

On thàinig gnè de thùr
O m' aois òige dhomh,
Nìor facas creutair dhiubh
Bu cho-glòrmhoire:
Bha Maili 's dearbha caoin,
'S a gruaidh air dhreach nan caor,
Ach caochlaideach mar ghaoith
'S i ro òranach;
Bha Peigi fad an aois—
Mur b' e sin b' i mo ghaol;
Bha Marsaili fìor aotrom
Làn neònachais;
Bha Lili a' taitne' rium
Mur b' e a ruisg bhith fionn;
Ach cha bu shàth bùrn-ionnlaid
Don Mhòraig s' iad.

Siubhal

No I don't care, I don't care
for any of them but Morag
whose elegance and dress
epitomize the whole *lass
o' pairts.* No ornament
collected can replace her
inner good, yet an ornament
no less, she's uncollectible,
even among that uncommon
prayer spanning Lewis to Mull.
She greets *Halò!*
with a human halo,
and from top to bottom
embodies perfect form.
Younger than her years
she'll luringly reach out
to spirit a touch
and be touched,
if you say please.
O, she's such
a tease.

Siubhal

O,'s coma leam,'s coma leam
Uil' iad ach Mòrag:
Rìbhinn dheas chulach
Gun uireas'aibh foghlaim;
Chan fhaighear a tional
Air mhaise no bhunailt,
No 'm beusaibh neo-chumanta
Am Muile no 'n Leòdhas;
Gu geamnaidh, deas, furanach,
Duineil, gun mhòrchuis,
Air thagha' na cumachd
O 'mullach gu 'bhrògaibh;
A neul tha neo-churraidh
'S a h-aigne ro-lurach,
Gu brìodalach, cuireideach,
Urramach, seòlta.

Siubhal

Give it up, give it up
for Morag, who in one wink
can tweak the boys to disobey
that silly *always*
of wedlock. To stretch out, lay
not only with her, but her treasure…
The pleasure was all mine.
Hot dreams of the body ravish.
Stalk and score.
Temptation is sick.
Yet right before my eyes
her neckline, candlelit: and I'm
consumed by
a whinfire of thought.

Siubhal

O guiliugag, guiliugag,
Guiliugag Mòrag!
Aice a ta 'chulaidh
Gu curaidh nan òigfhear;
B' e 'n t-aighear 's an sòlas
Bhith sìnte ri d' ulaidh
Seach daonnan bhith fuireach
Ri munaran pòsaidh.
Dam phianadh 's dam ruagadh
Le buaireadh na feòla,
Le aislingean connain
Na colna dam leònadh;
Nuair chithinn mu m' choinneimh
A cìochan le coinnil,
Thèid m' aign' air bhoilich
'S na theine dearg sòlais.

Siubhal

Hands down, hands down
Morag is the most snug
in Europe. A crotch thatched
and breasts
so whitewashed
would scandalize
the Pope.
Lily of the valley
her pigment,
but her breasts reappear
variously red, ready and set.
Ample in-hand
they ache
to be kneaded,
to know love alone
shirks all
blessing of clan and kin,
and in turn, you'll be needed then.
Your spirits renewed;
for as her desire grows
so do you…

Siubhal

O fairigean, fairigean,
Fairigean Mòrag!
Aice a ta 'chroiteag
As toite san Eòrpa;
A cìochan geal criostal,
Na' faiceadh tu stòit' iad
Gun tàirneadh gu beag-nàir'
Ceann-eaglais na Ròimhe;
Air bhuige 's air ghile
Mar lili na' lònan;
Nuair dhèanadh tu 'n dinneadh
Gun cinneadh tu deònach;
An deirgead, an grinnead,
Am mìnead 's an teinnead,
Gum b' àsainn chur-spionnaidh
Agus spioraid à feòil iad.

Ùrlar

Now let's raise the tone.
In the dawn of our abandon
Phoebus brightened the seas.
The deer-forest steamed
and deep in it, in the rutting,
our doe-and-roebuck chase
round saplings was dizzying,
the hill and spinney
of it all. We made love,
and we made love again,
again, fucked and flourished
till there was nothing
left to give, and finishing
we laughed together—
out of breath our laughter.

Ùrlar

Thogamaid ar fonn
Anns an òg-mhadainn,
'S Phebus a' dath nan tonn
Air fiamh òrainsean:
Far cèill' cha bhiodh conn
Air sgàth dhoire 's thom,
Sinn air dàireadh trom
Le 'r cuid gòraileis;
Dìreach mar gum biodh
Maoiseach 's boc à frìth
Crom-ruaig achèile dian
Timcheall òganan;
Chailleamaid ar clì
A' gàireachdaich leinn fhìn,
Le bras-mhacnas dian sin
Na h-ògalachd.

Siubhal

Delirium! Delirium
from her, a girl blonde,
lurid: how she snuffs out
her own flint-spark glow,
and in one white bite
hewn from snow.
As sex and excess,
as body and beauty,
so Dido, so Venus,
so Morag ravishes
my seasons,
my genius
spent.
A girl with sharp agency
can pierce the heart
clean through.

Siubhal

O dastram, dastram,
Dastram Mòrag!
Rìbhinn bhuidh', bhasdalach,
Leac-ruiteach ròsach;
A gruaidhean air lasadh
Mar an lasair-chlach dhathte,
'S a deud mar a' sneachda,
Cruinn-shnaighte 'n dlùth òrdugh;
Ri Venus cho tlachdmhor
An taitneachdainn fheòlmhor,
Ri Dido cho maiseach,
Cho snasmhor 's cho còrr rith';
'S e thionnsgain dhomh caitheamh
'S a lùghdaich mo ràithean,
A' bhallag ghrinn laghach
Chuir na gathan sa 'm fheòil-sa.

Siubhal

If I wasn't shackled,
keyless in wedlock, I'd lay
my inmost heart at Morag's altar,
her feet like a bridal stool's.
No regrets, no second thoughts
except to displease her
would equal death.
Respect. All my respect, Morag.
In the tease and heat
of a Sunday barely begun,
you licked me clean.
The blood turning in my veins:
my sin, your communion.

Siubhal

'S mur bithinn fo ghlasaibh,
Cruaidh-phaisgte le pòsadh,
Dh'ìobrainn cridhe mo phearsainn
Air an altair-se Mòraig;
Gun lìobhrainn gun airtneal
Aig stòlaibh a cas e,
'S mur gabhadh i tlachd dhiom
Cha b' fhad a sin beò mi.
O! 'n urram, an urram,
An urram do Mhòraig!
Cha mhòr nach do chuir i
M' fhuil uil' às a h-òrdugh,
Gun d' rug oirr' ceum-tuislidh
Fo imeachd mo chuislean,
Le teas is le murtachd
O mhochthrath Didòmhnaich.

Siubhal

Sidereal lass, cloudless you dazzle
in unfussy cool. In swansdown—
a smooth muted whiteout,
your waist. Cute nook
among waste. I mean it.
You are untouched earth,
if not a flourish of limbs—
nimble, intricate, tender. Fair
enough, sapling. You susurrate
instead of brag. Keep secrets
when you've been bad.

Siubhal

’S tu reula nan cailin,
Làn lainnir, gun cheò ort;
Fìor chòmhnard, gun charraid,
Gun arral, gun bheòlam;
Cho mìn ri clòimh eala,
’S cho geal ris a’ ghaillinn;
Do sheang-shlios sèimh fallain,
Thug barrachd air mòran.
’S tu Bànrigh nan ainnir,
Cha sgallais an còmhradh;
Àrd, foinnidh nad ghallan,
Gun bhallart, gun mhòrchuis;
Tha thu coileant’ nad bhallaibh,
Gu h-innsgineach, allamh;
Caoin, meachair’, farast’,
Gun fharam, gun ròpal.

Ùrlar

Free me, annul my word.
I have given more love
than I should,
but I would give more.
As love succumbs to madness
the strength to suffer
is outweighed.
A lover of madness then—
the madman
you have made of me.
You unmade me. You
taker of my heart, my resolve.
My undertaker,
you lay down over me
like clay in the kirkyard.

Ùrlar

B' fhèarr gum bithinn sgaoilt'
Às na còrdaibh sa;
Thug mi tuilleadh gaoil
Is bu chòir dhomh dhuit;
Gun tig fo dhuine taom,
Gu droch-ghnìomh bhios claon—
Cuireadh e cruaidh-shnaoim
Air on ghòraich sin:
Ach thug i seo mo chiall
Uile uam gu trian:
Chan fhaca mi riamh
Tional Mòraig seo.
Ghoid i uam mo chrìdh',
'S shlad i uam mo chlì,
'S cuiridh i sa chill
Fo na fòdaibh mi.

Siubhal

My question answered
by what I behold: a woman
whose breasts surrender
to white. Yours are turrets,
your nipples peace,
but my willingness
to thole the impossible
prospect of us
diminishes with each
minute lost. Your cherry
mouth candied mine, a kiss
vermillion as rose
and as red as Cupid's
swift-tipped arrows.
You left me
ruined, my coat
shot through.

Siubhal

Mo cheist agus m' ulaidh
De chonnairc mi d' sheòrs' thu,
Le d' bhroilleach geal-thuraid
Na' mullaichean bòidheach;
Chan fhaigh mi de dh'fhuras
Na nì mionaid uat fuireach,
Ged tha buarach na dunach
Dam chumail bho d' phòsadh.
Do bheul mar an t-sirist,
'S e milis ri phògadh,
Cho dearg ri bhermilion
Mar bhileagan ròsan:
Gun d' rinn thu mo mhilleadh
Le d' Chupid dam bhioradh,
'S le d' shaighdean caol biorach
A rinn ciorram fo m' chòta.

Siubhal

I notice sadness grows
with your absence, Morag.
The millstone of me launched below
the swelling sea drags
love's sailing.
No one in this whole world
rivals an otherworldly girl.
Your hair day-bright breaks the heart.
Its kinky curls, blowout of curls
and waves,
every ring and satin tress
uncoils, loops back as silken
rope fastened round my neck.
Swirls, jewelry, starch.
Yours are all the rage.

Siubhal

Tha mi làn mulaid
On chunnaic mi Mòrag;
Cho trom ri clach-mhuilinn
Air lunnaibh da seòladh:
Mac-samhailt na cruinneig
Chan eil anns a' chruinnidh;
Mo chrìdh' air a ghuin leat
On chunnaic mi d' òr-chùl
Na shlamagan bachallach,
Casarlach, còrnach;
Gu fàinneagach, cleachdagach,
Dreach-lùbach, glòrmhor;
Na reulagan cearclach
Mar usg'raichean dreachmhor,
Le fùdar san fhasan,
Grian-lasta, ciabh òr-bhuidh'.

Siubhal

Your edges soft
as bog cotton,
posh cinnamon
your kiss,
and the Phoenix
rarely rises in
a coat on-fleek
as yours is.
With happiness
only a lass has,
stuck-up nor staid,
you're more
flawless than
your flaws convey.
If you saw yourself
as I see you,
in Sunday's best
among the good-folk,
you might do
a double take:
you're heaven sent
with such shapes
and such gifts
as only God
could give are
without fail why
Earth is so bonny.

Siubhal

Do shlios mar an canach,
Mar chaineal do phògan,
Ri Phenix cho ainneamh
'S glan lainnir do chòta;
Gu mùirneanach, banail,
Gun àrdan, gun stannart,
'S i còrr ann an ceanal,
Gun ainnis, gun fhòtas.
Na' faicte mo leannan
Sa mhath-shluagh Didòmhnaich,
B' i coltas an aingil
Na h-earradh 's na còmhradh;
A pearsa gun talach,
Air a gibhtean tha barrachd,
An Tì a dh'fhàg thu gun aineamh
A rinn de thalamh rud bòidheach.

Ùrlar

Sick off the sweetmeat we make of each other...
When Mammon stands
oblique to man, his sleight of hand
and ours together
move seamlessly. We hold the body as love
and love the body in vain.
Daft as we are decadent,
we take for granted everything,
so I was convinced
till you so clearly rose to higher ground
where scale and excellence
are restored—
yours, Morag, yours:
the one fair god
to which I am drawn
with a cleft heart.
Long gone.

Ùrlar

Tha saoghal làn de smaointinnean feòlmhor,
Mamon bidh dar claonadh
Le ghoisnichean;
A' cholann bheir oirnn gaol
Ghabhail gu ro-fhaoin,
Air strìopachas, air craos
Agus stròdhalachd:
Ach cha do chreid mi riamh
Gun do sheas air sliabh
Aon tè bha cho ciatach
Ri Mòraig s';
A subhailcean 's a ciall
Mar gum biodh ban-dia,
Leagh i 'n crìdh am chliabh
Le 'cuid òrrachan.

Siubhal

You hide
your thoughts.
What good is done
holding your tongue—
a rare chanter
melody of a lilting girl,
equally rare in
mainland and isle.
Complete and comely
and soothing and sudden
as you are, my wife,
if she discovered us,
would bury me
alive: love severed,
all my worth worthless.
Still, no runoff
beyond Loch Shiel
and no snow atop
Cruachan's hind-field
starves this fire
of mind.

Siubhal

Ur comhairle na ceilibh orm,
Ciod eile a their no nì mi?
Mun rìbhinn bu tearc ceileireadh
A sheinneadh air an fhìdeig;
Chan fhaighear a leith'd eile seo
Air tir-mòr no 'n eileanaibh,
Cho iomlan is cho eireachdail,
Cho teiridneach 's cho bìogail.
'S nì cìnnteach gur nì deireasach,
Mur ceilear seo air Sìne,
Mi thuiteam an gaol leth-phàirteach,
'S mo cheathrannan am dhìobhail:
Chan eil de bhùrn an Seile siud,
No shneachd an Cruachan eilidneach,
Na bheir aon fhionnachd eiridneach
Don teine a ta nam innsgin.

Siubhal

All ears as my spirit,
charmed by your chanter, lifts
out toward the lyrical air
and with a spring in my step
I stepdance the *ùrlar*,
when your fingers take the lead
they take me down
the scale, swinging lower
to keep pace, a lower melody
freely arranged to a four-
three-two-one whole bass
drone… Wow! Execution,
commandment through *ceòl-mòr*,
through huge sudden sound,
a standing ovation as
the house is brought down
to its knees. A long sharp
delicate keen, then sullen trill
hypnotic, undisrupted,
warbling over broad hill
like thunder after a storm,
your footfall in time.
Even after your performance,
ever after: resonant, straight, true,
the *crùnluath* of your fingers,
ringing in my ears still.

Siubhal

Nuair chuala mi ceòl leadanach
An fheadain a bh' aig Mòraig,
Rinn m' aigne dannsa beadarach,
'S e freagra' dha le sòlas:
Sèimh-ùrlar socair, leadarra
A puirt, 's a meòir a' breabadaich;
B' e siud an oirfeid eagarra
Don bheus na creaga mòra.
Ochòin! A feadan bailleagach,
Cruaidh, sgailleagach, glan, ceòlmhor,
Nam binn-phort stuirteil, trileanta,
Rèidh, mion-dhìonach, bog, ro-chaoin;
A' màrsal còmhnard, stàiteil sin,
'S e lùthmhor, gràsmhor, caismeachdach,
Fìor chruinn-lùth brisg, spalparra,
F' a cliath-lùth bras-chaoin, spòrsail.

Siubhal

Heads turn and worship and study
this girl who delights in having eyes
all over her. Her chanter sings:
music to my ears. Improvisational flash.
Song-possessed fairy-licks
storm with bliss and intonation.
No surprise she's a formalist,
trained to stir you up
just to shut you down. Crazy how
one fingertap can skirl such a central tune.
Her most intricate pattern,
a musical star chart. Finger-fast attack,
clean, slick, effortless. Her
pinkie bursts off yet somehow plays on.
Dizzying, splendid curls of pipe song.

Siubhal

Chinn pròis is stuirt is spracalachd
Am ghnùis nuair bheachdaich guamag,
A' seinn an fheadain ioraltaich,
B' àrd iolach ann am chluasaibh;
A suain-cheòl, sìthe mireanach,
Mear-stoirmeil, pongail, mionaideach,
Na b' fhoirmeile nach sireamaid
Air mhireid, ri h-uchd tuasaid.
Om buille meòir bu lomarra
Gu pronnadh a' phuirt uaibhrich!
'S na h-uilt bu lùthmhor cromaidhean
Air thollaibh a' chruinn bhuadhaich;
Gun slaoid-mheòirich, gun rongaireachd,
Brisg, tioram, socair, collaideach;
Geal-lùdag nan geàrr-chollainnean,
Na' crap-lùth loinneil, guanach.

Ùrlar

Your hair,
interlace unending,
illuminates as I touch
and comb out the truth.
One tangible belief:
spirals, plaitwork
and insular rings
that lavishly uncurl
over your sharp brow.
Let's share more
wine, a brimful
to drink our thirst,
and we'll come down
hard on those holier-
than-thou: uncouth,
cool and *fuck all.*
Make for the spillway,
the glug of us
with each whisky,
tearing off old shirts
and everything just
to dress ourselves
in each other.

Ùrlar

Chaisgeamaid ar n-ìot'
Le glainn' fhìon a sin,
'S bhuaileamaid gu dian
Air glòir shìobhalta;
Tuilleadh cha bhiodh ann,
Gus an tigeadh àm
A bhith cluich air dam
Air na tìthean sin;
Dh'òlamaid ar dram,
Dh'fhògradh uainn gun taing,
Gach nì chuireadh maill'
Air bhith mìog-chuiseach;
Maighdean nan ciabh fann,
Shnìomhanach nan chlann;
Mala chaol, dhonn, cham,
Channach, fhìnealta.

Crùnluath

I left you and you left
a burr of whispers in my head,
a beehive of sex and nectar,
blocked up my nose
as I inhale lenten rose,
everything a blear
and so pained with squinting
I require a telescope.
Mountain and mite both
indistingushable to me,
inmate to my own body
and so pained with dreaming,
I worry what fortune
befalls the unfortunate.
Dead asleep then
from all that mental noise
suddenly I leap
into a joyous flash-
back, re-awakened by
my place between your legs...

Seven times, seven times
we drew from each other
a furious joy then peace of mind
felt nowhere else but the Fold.
Yet who do I discover there in bed
but Sìne, her grainy shock of blonde.
The woman I'd married all along.
Not you, Morag,
but almost-you. Her hand reaches
to coax me back up, to stroke

Crùnluath

Mo cheann tha làn de sheilleneaibh
O dhealaich mi ri d'bhrìodal,
Mo shòrn tha stopte a dh'elebor,
Na deil, le teine diombais;
Mo shùilean tha cho deireasach
Nach faic mi gnè gun telescop,
Is ged bhiodh meudachd beinnidh ann
'S ann theirinn gura frìd' e.
Dh'fhalbh mo chèidse corporra
Gu dochaireach le bruadar,
Nuair shaoil mi fortan thachairt dhomh,
'S mi'm thorroichim air mo chluasaig;
Air dùsgadh às a' chaithream sin
Cha d'fhuair mi ach ion-faileas dheth,
An ionad na maoin bearraideach
A mheal mi gu seachd uairean.

Ach ciod thug mi gu glan fhaireachadh
Ach carachadh rinn Cluanag;
'S cò seo, o thùs, bu Mhòrag ann,
Ach Sìne an òr-fhuilt chuachaich;
Nuair thùr i gun do lagaich mi
'S gu feumainn rag chur stailcidh ann,
Gun d'rinn i draoidheachd cadail dhomh,
Rinn cruaidh fìor rag dam luaidh'.
Bha chleasachd sa cho fìnealta,
'S cho innleachdach mun cuairt dhi,
Nach faodainn fhìn thaobh sìobhaltachd,
Gun dligheadh crìon thoirt uam dhi;
Gun thionndaidh mi gu h-òrdail rith',
'S gun shaoil mi gum b'i Mòrag i,

and strengthen the husband she loves:
not only thrust but one who must.
Through all her hex and hand
she raises her man, a standing stone.

I have to return a petty vow.
I have to turn over to her for now.
But I'll be thinking of you,
Morag. You the one
to receive my lips, through her:
a go-between, a means to an end.

'S gun d' aisig mi na pògan dhi
'S cha robh d' a còir dad uaith'.

Other Poems

Dream of the Prince

Here he comes now out of exile.
Our arms are wrapped in cloak and welcome.

His arrival thrills. This son of our rightful king
has looks to kill. A striking side view
with slick sword and plaited shield. My knight
in shining armor from overseas
is a tall, graceful rider whose caracole stuns any
light horse insurgence.
Rarest appearance, his skyful glare of March:
a rainbow's sklinter, the rain-grey rush.

One swing of that sword
would scythe our enemy, like an oat field.

bho Oran Do'n Phrionnsa

O, hì-rì-rì, tha e tighinn,
O, hì-rì-rì, 'n Rìgh tha uainn,
Gheibheamaid ar n-airm 's ar n-èideadh,
'S breacan-an-fhèilidh an cuaich.

'S èibhinn liom fhìn, tha e tighinn,
Mac an Rìgh dhlighich tha uainn,
Slios mòr rìoghail d'an tig armachd,
Claidheamh us targaid nan dual.

'S ann a' tighinn thar an t-sàile
Tha 'm fear àrd as àille snuadh,
Marcaich' sunndach nan steud-each
Rachadh gu h-eutrom 'san ruaig.

Samhuil an Fhaoillich a choltas,
Fuaradh froise 's fadadh-cruaidh;
Lann thana 'na làimh gu cosgairt
Sgoltadh chorp mar choirc' air cluain.

Dream of Victory

Beneath the pipe's baleful blast,
all under one banner, renewed spirit
unfurls, suffuses us: dispossessed

then enriched by the passion to run
the rabble out, and as the cannons call
each switchback and beinn respond

thunderously. Their coda rings our ears
and the earth cracks open… Poor lad
on that day, still in his fancy dress

or uniform. Coat as red as a fox.
What is that broken over his head?
A cocked hat, like charred cabbage.

bho Oran Do'n Phrionnsa

Torman do phìoba 's do bhrataich
Chuireadh spiorad bras 'san t-sluagh,
Dh' èireadh ar n-ardan 's ar n-aigne,
'S chuirte air a' phrasgan ruaig.

Tairneanach a' *bhomb* 's a' chanain
Sgoilteadh e 'n talamh le 'chruas,
Fhreagradh dhà gach beinn 's gach bealach,
'S bhodhradh a mhac-tall' ar cluas!

Gur mairg d'an èideadh 'san là sin
Còta grànd' de 'n mhàdur ruadh,
Ad bhileach dhubh us cocàrd innt'
Sgoiltear i mar chàl mu 'n cluais!

Trout

in close succession
riffed staccato
off water, and the water
like sunny glass shattered
with their joyousness.
Vivace they played
        a tablature of flies,
they broke nature's laws
in scales of light:
        agility bejeweled
gill-brilliant, blue.

bho Allt an t-Siùcair

Na bric a' gearradh shùrdag
Ri plubraich dhlùth le chèil',
Taobh-leumnaich mear le lùthchleas
Sa bhùrn, le mùirn ri grèin;
Ri ceapadh chuileag siùbhlach,
Le'm bristeadh lùthmhor fhèin:
Druim lann-ghorm 's ball-bhreac giùran
'S an lannair-chùil mar lèig.

The Stream

Sweetwater, crisp-white-
wine water,
clear water ringing-
clear, sparkling-
in-spate sweetwater
rapid like rapids crash,
every weed,
every watercress
clutches to the new
bank-rose and flourishes
as this stream
carries virtue
and virtue this stream:
red nor grey, but clearcut
renewal of spirit,
where two meadows meet.

bho Allt an t-Siùcair

Gur milis, brisg-gheal, bùrn-ghlan,
Meall-chùirneineach 's binn fuaim,
Bras-shruthain Allt an t-Siùcair,
Ri torman siùbhlach, luath;
Gach biolair 's luibh len ùr-ròis
A' cinntinn dlùth mu bhruaich,
'S e toirt dhaibh bhuadhan sùghmhor
Dhan t-subhachas man cuairt.

Bùrn tana, glan gun ruadhan,
Gun deathaich ruaim, no ceò,
Bheir anam-fàs is gluasad
D'a chluaineagan mu 'bhòrd;

Penis Bookmark

Luck
extends to you
a placeholder that
thousands of places
have been held by,
a good bookmark
triangle-tipped,
cut of cardstock
or wrinkled gloss,
a chanter-ish kiss
though sweet, fit
and durable and
enduringly sleek:
pure *joie de vivre*
only when we pick
up where we left off.

Moladh air Sàr-Bhod

Tha ball-ratha sìnte riut
A choisinn mìle buaidh:
Sàr-bhodh iallach acfhainneach
Rinn-gheur sgaiteach cruaidh
Ùilleach feitheach feadanach
Làidir seasmhach buan
Beòdha treòrach togarrach,
Nach diùltadh bog no cruaidh.

Acknowledgements

Thanks to *Acumen* and *Gutter* in which some of these pieces first appeared. Thanks also to Ionad Eòghainn MhicLachlainn at the University of Aberdeen for having me speak about this book at their conference 'Knots, thorns and thistles: challenges and successes of translating into and out of Gaelic and Irish'.

Thank you to the Poetry Book Society for recommending this collection. It is an honour, but more importantly, institutional support helps elevate the importance of Alasdair and Gaelic among the world's literary canon.

All my gratitude to those whose work, scholarship and assistance help brought this collection to light: Meg Bateman, Ronnie Black, Pàdraig MacAoidh, Rody Gorman, Gillebrìde MacMillan, Alan Riach, Michael Newton.

Thank you to Penny Horner and to the whole Ardnamurchan community as well its Historical And Heritage Association for hosting the launch of this collection.

Thanks to my wife, Lauren, and to my family, for their love and support.

Thanks lastly to Aaron Kent and to the whole Broken Sleep family for believing in this work and, in general, for supporting minority language literature. Broken Sleep gu bràth!

LEAG A-MACH DO MHÌ-SHUAIMHNEAS